THE WALLFLOWER

YAMATONADESHIKO SHICHIHENGE

9

Tomoko Hayakawa

TRANSLATED AND ADAPTED BY
David Ury

LETTERED BY
Dana Hayward

DEL REY

BALLANTINE BOOKS · NEW YORK

A Del Rey Trade Paperback Original

The Wallflower copyright © 2004 by Tomoko Hayakawa
English translation copyright © 2006 by Tomoko Hayakawa

Published in the United States by Del Rey Books, an imprint of The Random House Publishing Group, a division of Random House Inc., New York.

DEL REY is a registered trademark and the Del Rey colophon is a trademark of Random House, Inc.

Publication rights arranged through Kodansha, Ltd.

First published in Japan in 2004 by Kodansha Ltd., Tokyo, as *Yamatonadeshiko Shichihenge*.

ISBN 0-345-48527-0

Printed in the United States of America

www.delreymanga.com

9 8 7 6 5 4 3 2 1

Translator and adaptor—David Ury

Lettering and touchup—Dana Hayward

Cover Design—David Stevenson

Contents

A Note from the Author   iv

Honorifics   v

The Wallflower, volume 9   1

Bonus Manga   165

About the Creator   172

Translation Notes   173

Preview of Volume 10   176

A Note from the Author

♥ This is "Ten," the cutest little fella in the whole wide world. His full name is Tennosuke Hayakawa. He's a male Scottish Field Cat. He's a bit naughty and he has a knack for getting into trouble, but he's still a good boy.♥ Thanks to Ten, every day is full of love and happiness. Even scooping up his poop brings me joy.♥

—Tomoko Hayakawa

Honorifics

Throughout the Del Rey Manga books, you will find Japanese honorifics left intact in the translations. For those not familiar with how the Japanese use honorifics, and more important, how they differ from American honorifics, we present this brief overview.

Politeness has always been a critical facet of Japanese culture. Ever since the feudal era, when Japan was a highly stratified society, use of honorifics—which can be defined as polite speech that indicates relationship or status—has played an essential role in the Japanese language. When addressing someone in Japanese, an honorific usually takes the form of a suffix attached to one's name (example: "Asuna-san"), or as a title at the end of one's name or in place of the name itself (example: "Negi-sensei," or simply "Sensei!").

Honorifics can be expressions of respect or endearment. In the context of manga and anime, honorifics give insight into the nature of the relationship between characters. Many English translations leave out these important honorifics, and therefore distort the feel of the original Japanese. Because Japanese honorifics contain nuances that English honorifics lack, it is our policy at Del Rey not to translate them. Here, instead, is a guide to some of the honorifics you may encounter in Del Rey Manga.

-san: This is the most common honorific, and is equivalent to Mr., Miss, Ms., Mrs. It is the all-purpose honorific and can be used in any situation where politeness is required.

-sama: This is one level higher than "-san" and is used to confer great respect.

-dono: This comes from the word "tono," which means "lord." It is an even higher level than "-sama," and confers utmost respect.

-kun: This suffix is used at the end of boys' names to express familiarity or endearment. It is also sometimes used by men amongst friends, or when addressing someone younger or of a lower station.

-chan: This is used to express endearment, mostly toward girls. It is also used for little boys, pets, and even amongst lovers. It gives a sense of childish cuteness.

Bozu: This is an informal way to refer to a boy, similar to the English terms "kid" or "squirt."

Sempai/senpai: This title suggests that the addressee is one's "senior" in a group or organization. It is most often used in a school setting, where underclassmen refer to their upperclassmen as "sempai." It can also be used in the workplace, such as when a newer employee addresses an employee who has seniority in the company.

Kohai: This is the opposite of "sempai," and is used toward underclassmen in school or newcomers in the workplace. It connotes that the addressee is of a lower station.

Sensei: Literally meaning "one who has come before," this title is used for teachers, doctors, or masters of any profession or art.

[blank]: This is usually forgotten in these lists, but it is perhaps the most significant difference between Japanese and English. The lack of honorific means that the speaker has permission to address the person in a very intimate way. Usually, only family, spouses, or very close friends have this kind of permission. Known as *yobisute*, it can be gratifying when someone who has earned the intimacy starts to call one by one's name without an honorific. But when that intimacy hasn't been earned, it can be very insulting.

CONTENTS

Chapter 35   3
The Journey to Becoming a Lady [Part 1]

Chapter 36   43
The Journey to Becoming a Lady [Part 2]

Chapter 37   83
The Prince in Sheep's Clothing

Chapter 38   125
The Eye of the Storm

Bonus Chapter   165
I Met Kiyoharu!!!

KYOHEI TAKANO—
A STRONG FIGHTER, "I'M THE KING."

WALLFLOWER'S BEAUTIFUL
CAST OF CHARACTERS (?)

TAKENAGA ODA—
A CARING FEMINIST.

RANMARU MORII—
A TRUE LADIES' MAN.

YUKINOJO TOYAMA—
A GENTLE, CHEERFUL
AND VERY EMOTIONAL GUY.

SUNAKO
NAKAHARA

SUNAKO IS A DARK LONER WHO
LOVES HORROR MOVIES. WHEN
HER AUNT, THE LANDLADY OF A
BOARDINGHOUSE, LEAVES TOWN
WITH HER BOYFRIEND, SUNAKO
IS FORCED TO LIVE WITH FOUR
HANDSOME GUYS. SUNAKO'S
AUNT MAKES A DEAL WITH THE
BOYS, WHICH CAUSES NOTHING
BUT HEADACHES FOR SUNAKO.
"MAKE SUNAKO INTO A LADY, AND
YOU CAN LIVE RENT FREE."

SUNAKO CONTINUES TO SEEK
SHELTER IN THE DARK RECESSES
OF HER ROOM. EVERYTHING
WILL BE FINE, AS LONG AS THE
LANDLADY DOESN'T FIND OUT.

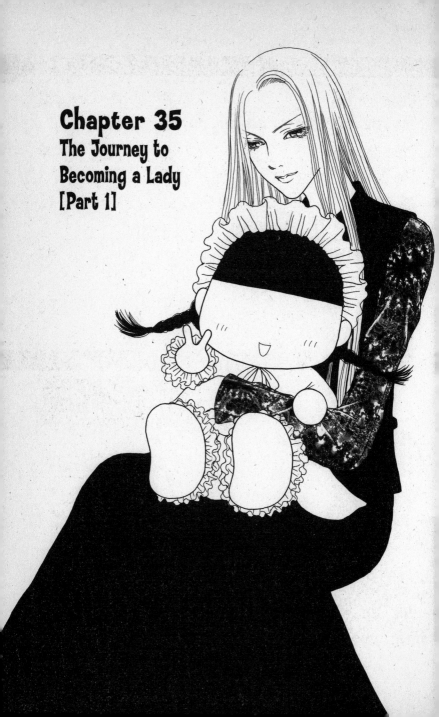

Chapter 35
The Journey to Becoming a Lady [Part 1]

RUMBLE RUMBLE

DON'T YOU GUYS HEAR THAT?

WHAT'S THAT WEIRD NOISE?

HUH?

THAT'S A "BEARY BIG BEAR"!

THUD.

On that day...

HA, HA, HA, HA, HA

HE LEFT THEM IN THE TRUNK.

I DON'T KNOW. WHY?

WHY COULDN'T THE ELEPHANT FIND HIS KEYS?

—4—

Nobody suspected that a terrible storm was heading...

...straight for the Nakahara household.

BEHIND THE SCENES

YOSSUI, WHOM I WROTE ABOUT IN BOOK 7, CAME BY TO HELP OUT THE OTHER DAY. ♥ (HIS NAME USED TO BE YOSHII.) (I KNEW HE WAS BUSY WITH HIS JOB, SO I STOPPED ASKING HIM TO WORK FOR ME, BUT THEN I FOUND OUT THAT HE QUIT. I CALLED HIM RIGHT AWAY. ♥) FROM NOW ON, YOSHII IS GONNA HELP ME ALL THE TIME. HE'S SO HELPFUL. ♥

AND GET THIS! HE WAS THE FIRST ONE TO STAY IN THE SPARE ROOM ← I USED TO ALWAYS SLEEP IN THAT SPARE ROOM. IN MY NEW APARTMENT. YOSHII WAS LIKE, "THERE'S A GHOST IN YOUR SPARE ROOM! A GHOST!" I HADN'T EVEN NOTICED. IT WAS JUST LIFE   AHH! BUT AS USUAL FOR ME....ACTUALLY, IT STILL IS! I GOT KIND OF SCARED,   IT'S A NEW BUILDING. SO EVERY TIME I HAD SOMEBODY OVER, I'D ASK IF THEY COULD FEEL THE PRESENCE OF A GHOST, BUT EVERYBODY WAS LIKE, "HOW SHOULD I KNOW?" COULD IT REALLY BE HAUNTED?

I'M HOME. ♥

きゃーははは
HA, HA, HA, HA

I THOUGHT YOU SAID WOOKIE!

HERE'S THE COOKIE.

HEY...

I THINK I'LL GO OUT SHOPPING WITH SUNAKO-CHAN.

HA, HA, HA, HA.

I HAVEN'T SEEN THEM IN AGES AND THEY JUST IGNORE ME.

HMMPH

OOPS, WE FORGOT TO CLEAN IT UP. ♥

HEY, LANDLADY! LAST NIGHT WE HAD A *PARTY* IN THIS ROOM. ♥

NICE, TAKENAGA!

CLEANING TIME! CLEANING TIME!

PANT PANT

SWIPE

RUMBLE

AWWW, SUNAKO-CHAN. YOU'RE THE CUTEST LITTLE GIRL IN THE WORLD. ♥

WHEN I GROW UP, I WANT TO BE JUST LIKE YOU, AUNTIE.

THANK YOU, AUNTIE. THANK YOU.

WHEN YOU GROW UP, WE'LL GO ALL KINDS OF PLACES TOGETHER, OKAY? ♥

I WAS HOPING WE WOULD BE JUST LIKE SISTERS....

WAIT, HOW OLD WAS SUNAKO-CHAN WHEN SHE SAID THAT?

HOW OLD IS THE LANDLADY, ANYWAY?

WHAT HAPPENED TO MY BEAUTIFUL DREAM?

I'M THROWING THIS GARBAGE AWAY! AHHH!

ぎゅ…
SQUEEZE

KYAAA!

FLASH

— 12 —

— 13 —

THERE'S NO WAY IN HELL I'M LETTING MY NIECE GO OUT WITH A GUY LIKE YOU

YOU'D BETTER BREAK IT OFF RIGHT NOW!

FRIENDSHIP
友情

I'LL GO ON VACATION WITH HER.

RA-RAN-MARU

GOOD LUCK, KYOHEI.

NO MATTER WHAT HAPPENS, DON'T GIVE UP.

YOU GUYS...

I DON'T WANT YOU GETTING A SORE THROAT. TAKE THESE.

I DON'T WANT YOUR TUMMY GETTING COLD. TAKE THIS.

Stomach Warmer

JUST TAKE IT.

WHAT IS IT?

?

TAKE THIS.

— 15 —

THIS IS THE REAL ME.

WHEN I'M NEXT TO THESE CREATURES OF THE LIGHT, I MELT.

AUNTIE...

I'M SORRY I NEVER TOLD YOU THE TRUTH, BUT...

SAY SOMETHING, BUDDY.

HAHH HAHH

SORRY, BUT I HAVE TO *RUN AWAY.*

OH, SO YOU CAN TALK TO HER, CAN YOU?

IT LOOKS LIKE THEY'RE GETTING ALONG FINE, MADAME.

YOU IDIOT.

BOING

KYAA!

CAN YOU BELIEVE THIS JERK? SAY SOMETHING TO ME, DAMN IT!

THE MADAME WAS USING THIS AS A SECOND HOME.

カチャ……. CLICK

I HAVE A MESSAGE FOR YOU FROM THE MADAME.

SUNAKO-SAMA.

THE ONLY THING IN HERE IS A BED!

WHAT'S WITH THIS ROOM?

THERE'S A TWO-WAY MIRROR IN THERE!

DON'T GO IN THE BATH-ROOM!

I HATE MIRRORS.

WHAT ABOUT THE OTHER ROOMS?

WHOOSH

SIGH, OH BROTHER...

FWUMP

PANT, PANT

HUH?

VWIIN

PLOP

PLOP

PLOP

A REVOLVING BED?

— 20 —

...DO IT WITH SUNAKO-CHAN.

CLICK

ARE YOU FIGHTING?

NO.

HELP ME, DORAEMON!

YOU IDIOT!

BESIDES, NOW WE'LL FINALLY GET TO *LIVE RENT FREE!*

MAYBE.

THERE'S ONLY ONE WAY OUT OF THAT ROOM.

AND YOU'D NEVER GET PAST SECURITY ANYWAY.

EVEN YOU CAN'T BREAK THROUGH THAT GLASS.

H-HOW THE HELL AM I SUP- POSED TO DO THAT...

I'M NOT RANMARU, YOU KNOW.

THINK ABOUT IT.

IT'S KYOHEI! IT'S ALMOST LIKE HE'S ON THE RADIO.

HOW RUDE.

AND I'LL ONLY WATCH ONE SLASHER FLICK PER DAY.

I'LL BRUSH MY HAIR.

I PROMISE THAT FROM NOW ON, I'LL TAKE A BATH AT LEAST ONCE EVERY THREE DAYS.

AUNTIE...

SO PLEASE...

LET ME OUT OF HERE!

SNIFFLE SNIFF

SNAP

— 25 —

GO TAKE A SHOWER!

IS THAT GOD-ZILLA?

%*&@#!!!

#$%...

THWUP

SLAM

YOINK
はしっ

SHIVER
ふる

ふる
SHIVER

BLUSH

WELL...

WELL, REMEMBER HOW QUICKLY HE FELL UNDER *HYPNOSIS* THAT ONE TIME?

I NEVER THOUGHT KYOHEI WOULD AGREE TO GO *ALONG WITH THIS* SO EASILY.

LET'S GIVE THEM *A LITTLE PRIVACY.* ♥

I DON'T WANNA HEAR ANY MORE!

HEARING YOUR FRIEND GET BUSY IS ABOUT AS GROSS AS IT GETS.

AHH, THIS IS SO EMBAR-RASSING!

THUD

I WONDER WHAT THEY'RE DOING IN THERE.

THUMP THUMP

COME ON...

— 39 —

Chapter 36
The Journey to Becoming a Lady [Part 2]

BEHIND THE SCENES

... (WHO'S CURRENTLY WORKING ON "BE LOVE") HELPED ME WITH THIS STORY ♥
...LLY ONLY CAME BY TO VISIT).

...AMAZING.
...G.

...DRAWINGS OF
...HEY CUTE? ♥
...HEY CUTE? ♥

...MADE ME AT
♥

... MACHIKO SAKURAI
...AND ME ABOUT TO
...PASS OUT FROM JOY.
...THANKS FOR YOUR
...HELP, SAKURAI. ♥

#SWIP

D-DRAW
A TRANS-
VESTITE
...

OKAY.

#SWIP

NOW...
DRAW
THE RICH
MADAM.

OKAY.

IF AI-CHAN-SENSEI OPENED AN OKONOMIYAKI RESTAURANT,
I'D BE THERE EVERY DAY. I REALLY DID PASS OUT.

GET ON YOUR HANDS AND KNEES.

OR 5 TIMES ON A GOOD DAY.

A NORMAL 15-YEAR-OLD BOY COULD HAVE DONE IT *TWICE* BY NOW!

ARE YOU A COMPLETE *IDIOT*? I GAVE YOU TWO WHOLE HOURS.

YOU'RE HER AUNT, HOW CAN YOU TALK LIKE THAT?

MISS LAND-LADY!

SLAM

I DON'T WANNA HEAR YOUR EXCUSES.

B-B-BUT I... I...

WAHH! CHECK OUT THIS ROOM!

AH...

THIS WAS YOUR IDEA, WASN'T IT?

THAT'S A PRETTY DIRTY TRICK... USING YUKI-CHAN LIKE THAT.

I LOVE THIS ROOM. ♥

YUKI...

KYOHEI DID THE BEST HE COULD!

IF YOU WANNA HIT SOMEONE, HIT ME! BUT LEAVE KYOHEI ALONE.

The landlady has a soft spot for Yuki.

GOOD WORK, KYOHEI.

KYRAA!

GOOD, NOW I CAN HIT YOU INSTEAD OF YUKI-CHAN.

SLAP SLAP SLAP

WHY DON'T YOU AND I MAKE USE OF THESE TOGETHER, MISS LANDLADY? ♥

HMMM...

HAS SUNAKO-CHAN COME TO?

...HAVEN'T BEEN TELLI—

ALL THIS TIME I...

I-I'M SORRY.

AUNTIE...

NO WAY!

SHUDDER SHUDDER
ガガガガ
ヮヮヮヮ

YOUR AUNT... ...SHOULD JUST GIVE UP ON ALL THIS "LADY" CRAP.

AUNTIE...

PARTY?

THAT LADY LOVES PARTIES.

ANOTHER ONE?

IF SHE KEEPS MAKING US HANG OUT WITH HER LIKE THIS, I'M NOT GOING TO THAT PARTY.

AND YOU CAN TELL HER THAT.

NO WAY. I DON'T WANNA GO!

EVERY SINGLE FREAKING DAY!

I'VE COME TO PICK YOU UP.

MORII-SAMA, ODA-SAMA...

DING
ピンポーン
DONG

おおおおおっ

WHOA!

I TOOK THE LIBERTY OF BRINGING THIS SMALL GIFT FOR SUNAKO-SAMA.

THE MADAME SAID IT WASN'T NECESSARY, BUT...

IT'S THE THIRD YEAR COMMEMORATION CEREMONY FOR HER DEARLY DEPARTED HUSBAND.

THE MADAM WAS VERY EXCITED ABOUT ATTENDING THE PARTY WITH SUNAKO-SAMA.

AUNTIE...

IT MUST BE NICE TO GO THROUGH LIFE WITH NO CONSCIENCE WHATSOEVER! WHEN IT COMES TO THE RENT, YOU'LL DO JUST ABOUT ANYTHING, WON'T YOU?

SHUT THE HELL UP!

WHAT CHOICE DID I HAVE? YOU THINK I WANTED TO GO AFTER YOU LIKE THAT?

BESIDES, I THOUGHT YOUR MOTTO WAS "IF I DON'T LIKE IT, I DON'T DO IT."

WHY DON'T YOU JUST TELL YOUR AUNT THE TRUTH?

GURGL

— 59 —

FLUMP

WE'RE SORRY.

HE SURE KNOWS HOW TO DRINK.

HOW DREAMY.

ISN'T HE JUST GOR-GEOUS?

SHUT UP! GO DRINK SOME WATER!

I WAS JUST TRY-ING TO ENJOY A COUPLE OF DRINKS. WHY THE HELL'D YOU HAVE TO GET IN MY WAY?

AUNTIE...!!

STUPID JERK.

I ALREADY HAVE!

SUNAKO SAID SHE DIDN'T WANNA GO, SO WHY DON'T YOU JUST GIVE UP?

I GUESS SHE WAS REALLY SAD THAT SHE COULDN'T COME TO THE PARTY WITH HER CUTE LITTLE NIECE.

YOU GOT HERE JUST IN TIME.

SHE'S GETTING TOTALLY OUT OF HAND.

WHY DON'T YOU QUIT MOVING ON FROM GUY TO GUY, AND...

...JUST PICK ONE AND STICK WITH HIM.

BECAUSE...

THE ONLY MAN I EVER TRULY LOVED IS ALREADY DEAD!

I'VE KNOWN HER *WAY WAY* LONGER THAN YOU HAVE.

GOD, YOU DON'T HAVE TO TELL ME THAT!

I *KNOW YOU* HAVE.

THIS ISN'T WORTH FIGHTING OVER.

GRR

SLAP

SLAP

SNAP

SHE DOES ALL THE CHORES AT HOME AND EVERY-THING.

I MEAN, GIVE HER A BREAK...

ALLOW
ME.

STARE

YOINK
YOINK
ふる
ふる

はあっ
はあっ
はあっ
PANT
PANT
PANT

TIME TO HIT THE SACK

YAWN
ふっ

HUH? WAS THE CURTAIN OPEN LIKE THAT...?

I-I DON'T WANNA KNOW. I DON'T WANNA KNOW.

WH-WHAT ARE YOU DOING SUNAKO-CHAN...

I'M NOT LOOKING.

YOU'RE LATE!

COULD THEY BE ANY LESS SUBTLE ...

CHATTER

CHATTER

AREN'T THEY HANDSOME.

ALL FOUR OF THEM.

FWISH

— 76 —

WHY EVEN BOTHER DRESSING LIKE THAT IF YOU'RE JUST GONNA COVER YOUR-SELF UP WITH THAT CURTAIN?

YOU DON'T LOOK ANY WORSE THAN THE LANDLADY, YOU KNOW?

SQUIRT

SHE SAID SHE JUST WANTED TO BE ABLE TO STAND NEXT TO HER AUNT WITHOUT EMBARRASSING HER.

SUNAKO-CHAN BEGGED US TO HELP DRESS HER UP.

THAT'S RIGHT ...

HELLO, EVERYBODY. I'M TOMOKO HAYAKAWA.

HERE'S A LIST OF MY RECENT ACTIVITIES. IT'S ALL ABOUT CONCERTS, SO PLEASE FEEL FREE TO SKIP IT IF YOU'RE NOT INTERESTED. ACTUALLY, I HAVEN'T BEEN TO MANY CONCERTS LATELY ... I'M SURPRISED MYSELF.

SMAP SEE CHAPTER 38. I HAD SO MUCH FUN. I'D LOVE TO GO AGAIN SOMETIME WITH AI-CHAN-SENSEI. ♥

BAROQUE THEY HAD A CONCERT AT THE BUDOUKAN. ♥ WOW, THEY'VE REALLY MADE IT BIG! AS ALWAYS, BANSAKU-KUN (BASS) WAS TOO COOL! ♥ DURING THE INTERMISSION, I WAS TALKING TO REI-KUN'S (VOCALS) FRIEND, AND SHE WAS LIKE "I SAW YOU GIVE A PRESENT TO BANSAKU-KUN, GOOD FOR YOU. ♥" I GUESS SHE WAS WATCHING ME. I WAS SO EMBARRASSED... SHE SAID SHE READS MY MANGA...

ZEN'S DEAD STOCK TOY MY FRIEND YUKI-KUN (DRUMS) JOINED THIS BAND AS A BACK UP MEMBER, SO I WENT TO SEE THEM. ZEN-KUN (VOCALS) STARTED THIS BAND AFTER VANILLA BROKE UP. I HAD SO MUCH FUN. I HOPE THEY KEEP PLAYING TOGETHER. ♥

MICHIRU-KUN EVENT I WENT TO SEE THIS EVENT BECAUSE TORU-SAN'S (MOI DIX MOIS, KIREEK) BAND AND HITOKI-KUN (EX KUROYUME ♥♥♥) WAS CO-HEADLINING, AND ALSO YUKI-KUN HAPPENED TO BE WORKING THE EVENT. I HAD LOTS OF FUN. ♥ THANKS, TORU-SAN, MICHIRU-KUN, AND YUKI-KUN.

MIYAVI WOW, MASA-KUN IS SUCH A HOTTIE. HE'S TALL, AND HE'S CUTE EVEN WITHOUT MAKEUP. I GOT A LITTLE NERVOUS WHEN HE SHOOK MY HAND WITH HIS BIG HAND. I GOT TO SPEAK WITH PATA-SAN (EX X JAPAN) AND SHINYA-KUN (EX LUNA SEA) AT THE CONCERT. ♥ I WAS SO HAPPY, ALTHOUGH I WAS A LITTLE NERVOUS. ♥ SHINYA-KUN LOOKED EXACTLY LIKE HE DOES ON TV. ♥ PATA-SAN WAS SUCH A NICE PERSON. LOVE ♥ I SPOTTED DAIGO-KUN (DAIGO STARDUST) THERE TOO. HE WAS SO HOT THAT I COULDN'T STOP STARING AT HIM... FROM A DISTANCE, OF COURSE.

HUH? IS THAT IT? NO WAY... WELL, I DID GO SEE SHOCKING LEMON AND GENTLE AS USUAL, BUT...

I GUESS I DIDN'T GO OUT MUCH BECAUSE I DIDN'T WANT TO LEAVE MY LOVELY KITTY ALONE IN THE HOUSE. (SEE BONUS PAGES.) I WAS REALLY BUSY WITH WORK TOO.

ACTUALLY, TOMORROW ♥♥♥ I'M GOING TO SEE *KIYOHARU-SAMA* AT *SHIBUYA KOUKAIDO* ♥♥♥ I'M SO EXCITED. ♥ KYAA. KYAA. KYAA.

I HOPE BAROQUE'S CONCERT SCHEDULE COMES OUT BY THE TIME THIS BOOK GOES ON SALE.

Chapter 37
The Prince in Sheep's Clothing

HRRMPH . . .

WITHOUT THESE PICKLES, I CAN'T MAKE TARTAR SAUCE.

EVEN WITH MY SUPER STRENGTH, I CAN'T OPEN IT.

This is the shopping district in Kyohei Takano's hometown.

It was a lively thriving area while Kyohei lived there, but it is now nearly abandoned.

HYUU

I WONDER WHAT HE'S UP TO?

I WONDER HOW TAKANO-KUN IS DOING?

BEHIND THE SCENES

A FEW DAYS BEFORE MY DEADLINE, I WENT TO JUDGE A MODELING AUDITION FOR THE H.NAOTO CLOTHING LINE. I'M HORRIBLE AT TALKING IN FRONT OF PEOPLE (I JUST CAN'T DO IT). IT WAS A VERY LAID-BACK ENVIRONMENT, BUT I WAS STILL TOTALLY NERVOUS. HOW LAME.

THE MODELS WERE ALL SO CUTE. ♥ THEY WERE DEFINITELY THE MODELS OF THE FUTURE. ♥ AND THEY WERE ALL SO NICE. ♥♥♥ THEY WERE PROBABLY EVEN MORE NERVOUS THAN I WAS, BUT THEY REALLY HELPED CALM ME DOWN. THANKS. ♥ I WAS SO HAPPY TO GET TO TALK TO NAOTO-SAN (I'M A HUGE FAN. ♥). THANKS FOR EVERYTHING. AND THANKS TO THE STYLIST AND THE PHOTOGRAPHER. I ONLY GOT TO TALK TO THE GUESTS FOR A LITTLE BIT, BUT I WAS STILL REALLY HAPPY...

A WEEK BEFORE MY DEADLINE, I WENT TO MY FRIEND'S WEDDING. IT WAS SO FUN. ♥ CONGRATULATIONS, HEE-SAN. ♥ GOOD LUCK WITH YOUR NEW BRIDE. ♥

BUT YOU'VE GOT YOUR OWN UNIQUE THING GOING ON, YUKI.

HUH?

SCREW THAT! I WANNA BE COOL.

IS THAT SUP-POSED TO CHEER ME UP?

THAT'S OKAY, YUKI. AT LEAST YOU'RE CUTE.

AND YOU LOOK GREAT IN DRAG.

YEAH, AND WHEN WE WENT TO EAT TAKOYAKI, YOU WERE THE ONLY ONE WHO GOT A DIS-COUNT.

KIDS AND ANIMALS LOVE YOU.

OLD FOLKS DO TOO.

YOU'RE SO CUTE THAT NO ONE CAN EVER STAY MAD AT YOU.

HUH?

ARE YOU GUYS TWINS? YOU LOOK EXACTLY ALIKE.

LOOK AT THIS PICTURE. IS THIS YOUR LITTLE BROTHER AND SISTER?

NOW YOU'RE JUST MAKING FUN OF ME.

I AM NOT!

THAT'S WAY MORE IMPORTANT THAN BEING "COOL."

JUST LOOK AT ALL THE LETTERS THEY SENT YOU.

A-AND YOUR FAMILY LOVES YOU.

THERE'S NOTHING COOL ABOUT THAT.

IT'S TOO
LATE FOR
THAT.

WE CAN'T
JUST SIT
BY AND
WATCH
OUR CITY
DIE.

I'M
AFRAID
THAT'S
NOT AN
OPTION.

LET'S JUST
FORGET
ABOUT
TAKANO-
KUN.

BUT I
THOUGHT WE
DECIDED TO
START OVER
FROM
SCRATCH.

SO...

THIS IS
WHERE
TAKANO-
KUN
LIVES.

YEAH,
IT'S HIS
FAULT FOR
SLEEPING
THROUGH
DINNER.

LET'S EAT
KYOHEI'S
TOO.

ZZZ

KYO-
HEI.

DINNER'S
READY.

AFTER
ALL THE
TROUBLE
I WENT
THROUGH
...

OH, KYOHEI, YOU'RE UP.

I'M GOING TO THE CONVENIENCE STORE. NEED ANYTHING?

OH, I'LL GO WITH YOU.

TO BUY A BENTO.

SINCE I MISSED DINNER.

...

CLICK

....

I CAN'T BELIEVE THEY DIDN'T WAKE ME UP.

GRUMBLE

DING

SHOCK

AND WATCH OUT FOR CARS.

STAY OUT OF DARK ALLEYS.

CALL ME IF ANYTHING HAPPENS.

I'M NOT A LITTLE KID.

WELL, I GUESS I'LL GO BY MYSELF.

— 90 —

SNIFFLE
SNIFF

OH, YOU MUST BE A FRIEND OF HIS.

HOP IN.

KYOHEI...
KYOHEI...

SNIFFLE
SNIFF
SNIFF

HEY, THERE'S A PERSON OVER THERE.

— 105 —

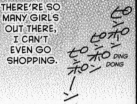

THE PHONE NEVER STOPS RINGING.

THAT RACKET IS DRIVING ME CRAZY.

THERE'RE SO MANY GIRLS OUT THERE, I CAN'T EVEN GO SHOPPING.

MY PAR- ENTS...

I'M SORRY, KYOHEI.

I DON'T EVEN HAVE A HOME THERE ANY- MORE.

...ARE MUCH BETTER OFF WITHOUT ME.

I WANT TO BE A GOOD MOTHER, BUT I'M JUST SO TIRED.

HOW CAN I GO BACK?

THAT'S WAY MORE IMPORTANT THAN BEING "COOL."

TAKANO

SLURP
ズ......

SHE SAID
SHE'S A
FRIEND OF
KYOHEI'S.

KYOHEI
LOOKED
AS GOOD
AS EVER.

OH,
THAT
BOY...

NO WAY!

ARE YOU HURT?

ARE YOU OKAY, YUKI?

LOOKS LIKE YOU SKINNED YOUR NOSE.

I'M FINE.

I SAVED KYOHEI!

POUT
む

YOUR CUTE FACE WON US OVER. WE JUST COULDN'T BEAR TO SEE YOU SAD.

ぽん
PLOP

WHATEVER! JUST LAY OFF THE DEVIL WORSHIP.

BUT WE HAVEN'T GIVEN UP YET.

ふふふふふ
HEH HEH   HEH HEH

BECAUSE OF YOUR FRIEND HERE, WE'LL LET YOU GO THIS TIME.

TAKANO-KUN.

GEEZ, MAN... DON'T GET TOO CRAZY...

KYOHEI!

YUKI!

...THEY PUT KYOHEI IN.

THIS IS DEFINITELY THE CAR...

TAKE-NAGA!

RAN-MARU!

Chapter 38
The Eye of the Storm

KYOHEI AT AGE 3

YEAH, WASN'T HE CUTE?

BUT HE WAS STILL A BISHONEN.

CAN YOU BELIEVE HE WAS ONLY IN KINDER-GARTEN?

CHECK OUT THAT LOOK IN HIS EYE.

ぎゃはははは
BWA HA HA HA HA

ぎゃはははは
BWA HA HA HA
HE HASN'T CHANGED A BIT.

RIGHT AFTER THAT TAKANO-KUN CRASHED HIS TRICYCLE RIGHT INTO ME. I WAS *BADLY INJURED.*

I TOOK A PICTURE OF HIM PLAYING WITH MY SON.

HE WAS SO CUTE.

HUH?

IT'S OKAY. YOUR DAD TOOK HER HOME WITH HIM, TAKANO-KUN.

I'M GOING TO LOOK FOR SUNAKO NAKAHARA.

STOP WASTING TIME.

♣ BEHIND THE SCENES ♣

I WROTE THIS STORY IN AUGUST. I WENT TO OSAKA TO SEE MY (FIRST) SMAP CONCERT. ♥ AI-CHAN-SENSEI (SHE LIVES IN OSAKA) HAD AN EXTRA TICKET AND SHE GAVE IT TO ME. THANKS AI-CHAN ♥♥♥

I WENT THERE HOPING TO SEE NAKAI-KUN, BUT I ENDED UP GOING CRAZY OVER KIMURA-KUN. ♥ TAKUYA KIMURA IS TOTALLY HOT! IT WAS MY FIRST TIME USING A PENLIGHT. THEY'RE REALLY FUN. YOU CAN READ ALL ABOUT THE DETAILS OF THAT DAY ON AI-CHAN-SENSEI'S HOMEPAGE. (IT'S ALL TRUE!)

THE WEEK AFTER THE SMAP SHOW, I WENT TO SEE BAROQUE AT THE BUDOUKAN CONCERT HALL. ♥ BANSAKU-KUN IS SO, SO, SO COOL. ♥♥♥ I WROTE THIS STORY WHILE GOING CRAZY OVER TAKUYA KIMURA AND BANSAKU-KUN. BUT THE STORY HAS NOTHING TO DO WITH THEM ...

CHECK OUT THE ENTRY FOR AUGUST 22ND, 2003.

SIGH

HIS WHOLE FAMILY IS PROBABLY *BLINDINGLY BRIGHT!*

THIS IS THE FORMER HOME OF THAT *CREATURE OF THE LIGHT.*

I WAS LURED HERE BY THAT DEMON FACE, BUT...

WHAT THE HECK AM I THINKING?

AH

I'VE GOTTA GET OUT OF HERE.

SHIVER

I-IF THEY GET THE WHOLE FAMILY TOGETHER, THEN... THEN...

...AREN'T CREATURES OF THE LIGHT AT ALL. ♥

HIS MOM AND DAD...

WAIT, YOUR ROOM IS—

HEY, WAIT.

FINE, I'LL STAY THE NIGHT.

AH

YOINK

WHO THE HELL DO YOU THINK YOU ARE?

I'LL HITCHHIKE.

YOU DON'T HAVE ENOUGH MONEY TO GET HOME.

WAIT!

WELL, I'LL BE LEAVING NOW....

I'LL TAKE DEATH ANY DAY!!!

UM...

SIGH

FWUP

ARE YOU TRYING TO KILL ME?!

B-BUT IT'S YOUR HOUSE.

LOOK, I DON'T WANNA BE HERE ANY MORE THAN YOU DO!

SHUT UP! BECAUSE THIS IS THE ONLY ROOM, THAT'S WHY!

BUT WHY DO WE HAVE TO SLEEP IN THE SAME ROOM?

I'M GOING HOME.

YOU CAN'T GO HOME.

QUIT BEING SO STUBBORN.

YOU LITTLE—

WHOOSH

L-LET GO OF ME!

AH!

I CAN'T STAND BEING NEAR A CREATURE OF THE LIGHT LIKE YOU!

I'LL DIE.

I—

DRIP DRIP

HMMPH

WHACK

KYAAA!

HE LOOKS GOR-GEOUS AS ALWAYS.

WELL...

HOW CAN ANYBODY BE SO GOR-GEOUS?

MY SENTI-MENTS EXACTLY.

ドキドキドキドキ
THUMP
THUMP

AH, Y-YOU'RE UP.

I GUESS YOU'RE RIGHT.

I KNOW SHE'S A LITTLE STRANGE, BUT WHAT CAN WE DO?

H-HONEY, IT'S THAT FRIEND OF KYOHEI'S.

ギロリ
GLARE

ひーーーっ
AHHH

THERE'S NO WAY IN HELL I CAN SLEEP IN THE SAME ROOM WITH HIM.

I DON'T THINK SHE'S QUITE LIKE KYOHEI, HONEY.

HOW MANY PEOPLE HAVE *BEEN COMMITTED* BECAUSE OF YOU?

YEAH, I KNOW JUST WHAT YOU MEAN.

WH- WHAT A STRANGE GIRL.

SO HOW IS KYOHEI DOING?

OH, SO YOU'RE NAKA-HARA-SAN.

YOU DO?

BEATS ME.

HE'S SO BLINDINGLY BRIGHT, I CAN'T EVEN LOOK AT HIM.

HUH?

KYOHEI'S OLDER BROTHER IS NOTHING LIKE THAT. HE'S ALREADY MOVED OUT THOUGH...

I JUST DON'T KNOW HOW YOU AND I MANAGED TO GIVE BIRTH TO A GORGEOUS BOY LIKE HIM.

KYOHEI GOT INTO SO MANY FIGHTS, WE WERE ALWAYS HAVING TO DEAL WITH THE POLICE.

AND THE PHONE NEVER STOPPED RINGING.

EVERY DAY, GIRL AFTER GIRL WOULD SHOW UP AT OUR DOOR.

INTENSE

AND IT WAS JUST ME AND KYOHEI ALONE IN THIS HOUSE.

— 146 —

— 149 —

DIS-APPEAR, HUH?

I WISH HE'D JUST DISAPPEAR!

めむ...っ

CRACK

I-I CAN'T HELP IT...

I-IS THAT HOW YOU ALWAYS USED TO TALK TO KYOHEI?

めき めき
CRACK CRACK

BUT HE WAS ONLY IN JUNIOR HIGH.

めき めき
CRACK CRACK

KYAAA!

ふーう。
SIGH

YANK

ガコ
YANK

ポイ
PLOINK

WHAT THE HECK ARE YOU DOING?

ポイ
PLOINK

ポイ
PLOINK

ポイ
PLOINK

KYAA! QUIT IT!

YOU SEE...

I ACTUALLY SAW HER LAST NIGHT.

IT REALLY IS A GHOST!

I-IT VANISHED!

FWAH

SHE LEFT THOSE MEN IN A *POOL OF THEIR OWN BLOOD.*

AFTER TAKANO-KUN WAS KIDNAPPED, A *GIRL'S SPIRIT* APPEARED.

IT MUST'VE BEEN A SNAKE DEMON.

KYAAA!

WE PROMISE TO STAY AWAY FROM HIM! JUST LET US GO!

WE'RE SORRY! WE'RE SORRY!

THOSE GIRLS ARE ALL GONE!

H-HONEY!

...MY FAVORITE CHANEL PERFUME.

THIS IS...

TH—
THAT'S NOT WHAT I WAS TRYING TO SAY.

PAT PAT PAT

HEY.

HOW ABOUT SOME CASH FOR THE TRAIN?

KYOHEI.

THIS IS YOUR HOME.

I THOUGHT IT MIGHT MAKE HER FEEL BETTER.

I-I WAS PUTTING ALL HER MIRRORS INTO A BAG.

ドキ
SHOCK

WHAT WAS ALL THAT RACKET YOU WERE MAKING?

....

TCH. SHE'LL NEVER CHANGE.

WHY DIDN'T YOU JUST BREAK THEM? DIDN'T WANNA SEEM RUDE?

I'M USED TO HEARING THAT KIND OF CRAP FROM HER.

IT'S TRUE. SHE IS BETTER OFF WITHOUT ME.

I WONDER WHICH IS FASTER, GOING BY TRAIN OR BY CAR?

THE TRAIN, OF COURSE.

NOTHING.

WHAT'S WRONG, KYOHEI?

IF WE BEAT YOU HOME, YOU HAVE TO BUY US ALL RAMEN, KYOHEI.

BYE.

YOU HATE BEING AROUND ME TOO, DON'T YOU?

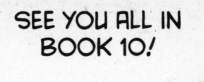

SEE YOU ALL IN BOOK 10!

HERE COMES THE BONUS MANGA.

AND MORE OF HAYAKAWA'S BABBLING.

IN THIS STORY, TOMOKO HAYAKAWA'S *DREAM COMES TRUE.*

IT WAS THE BIGGEST EVENT OF HER ENTIRE LIFE.

I MET KIYOHARU!!!

I GOT AN OFFER TO WRITE A BONUS MANGA FOR THIS ISSUE, BUT I'M A LITTLE NERVOUS ABOUT SHARING THIS EXPERIENCE.

UNINTELLIGIBLE SCREAMS OF JOY

$%¢
$@#
¢@^
*#!

KABOOM
どかーん

MY EARS HURT.

ONE DAY IN SEPTEMBER, I RECEIVED A CALL FROM THE *BESSATSU FRIEND* EDITING DEPARTMENT.

THE MAGAZINE "ZY" WANTS YOU TO DO AN **INTERVIEW WITH KIYOHARU.**

I FIGURED THIS MIGHT BE MY ONLY CHANCE, SO I HAPPILY ACCEPTED THE OFFER.

HEY, TOMOKO HAYAKAWA! YOU'RE NOT EVEN FAMOUS YET, ARE YOU SURE YOU'RE READY TO INTERVIEW KIYOHARU?

SOMEDAY I'M GONNA BE SUPER FAMOUS, AND I'LL EVEN GET TO INTERVIEW KIYOHARU!

IT WAS MY **LIFE-LONG DREAM.**

INTERVIEWING KIYOHARU... ALTHOUGH I'D FANTASIZED ABOUT IT SO MANY TIMES I NEVER IMAGINED THAT IT COULD ACTUALLY HAPPEN...

SCRIBBLE

SCRIBBLE

I WAS STILL IN A DREAMLIKE STATE, SO I JUST KEPT *TALKING AND TALKING.*

KIYOHARU-SAMA WAS SCHEDULED TO DO A PHOTO SHOOT AFTERWARDS, SO THE INTERVIEW TOOK PLACE AT A STUDIO IN AZABU.

THE DAY OF THE INTERVIEW, H-SAMA CAME ALONG WITH ME.

YOU MUST BE SO HAPPY.

*THEY PROBABLY CHOSE HER BECAUSE SHE'D ALREADY SEEN ME GO CRAZY AROUND KIYOHARU.

MY EDITOR M-SAMA

SHUDDER SHUDDER

EVERY-THING YOU SAY IS GONNA BE PUT IN PRINT.

THIS IS AN OFFICIAL INTER-VIEW.

YOU CAN'T GO COMPLETELY NUMB EITHER, OKAY?

YOU CANNOT FAINT, OKAY?

AND THEN...!

I JUST GOT A CAT.

SHE WAS SERIOUSLY WORRIED.

EVEN AFTER I'D STARTED THE INTERVIEW, I WAS TOO NERVOUS TO LOOK HIM IN THE EYE. I KEPT STARING AT THE FLOOR. OF COURSE, THE CONVERSATION WAS *GOING NOWHERE*.

FROZEN
コッチーン

ぐだぐだ。

BLAH BLAH

THE WRITER FROM THE MAGAZINE. SHE WAS SO BEAUTIFUL. SHE KIND OF RESEMBLED BANSAKU-KUN FROM BAROQUE.

I COULD BARELY SAY HELLO.

PULL YOUR-SELF TO-GETHER!

I'M SO SORRY.

OH MY.

マ〜マ〜

UH... UH... UH...

BUT, HE'S RIGHT IN FRONT OF ME.

...TRIED TO LOOK AT HIM FACE TO FACE.

I DECIDED TO BE BRAVE, AND...

NICE TO MEET YOU.

OH MY GOD, HE WAS BEYOND GOR-GEOUS!

KIYOHARU-SAMA ARRIVED! YEP! FOR REAL!

HIS OUTFIT WAS REALLY CUTE.

↙

どぇぇぇぅ

SQUIRT

H-H-HE'S JUST SMOKING LIKE ANY-BODY ELSE.

OKAY, KIYOHARU-SAMA IS JUST A *NORMAL* GUY.

IT WAS TIME FOR KIYOHARU-SAMA'S *PHOTO SHOOT.* ♥

WHILE HE WAS SHOOTING, I KEPT APOLOGIZING TO NORISUE-SAMA, THE BEAUTIFUL WRITER.

THANK GOD SHE WAS SO NICE.

THE INTERVIEW (IF YOU CAN CALL IT THAT) WAS FINALLY OVER, AND...

I TRIED TO IMAGINE THAT HE WAS JUST ANOTHER FRIEND OF MINE.

IT'S IT'S YUKI-TAA-KUN/CHAN!

→

THIS ISN'T KIYO-HARU.

DON'T LOOK. DON'T LOOK.

WHAT THE HELL AM I DOING HERE?

STARE

I'M MUCH MORE COMFORTABLE LIKE THIS. (WHAT AM I, A STALKER?)

I WATCHED THE WHOLE PHOTO SHOOT WHILE HIDING BEHIND A WALL.

I WAS ABOUT TO *EXPLODE!*

HE TALKED TO ME DURING THE SHOOT.

AREN'T YOU SLEEPY?

I'M SLEEPY.

IT WAS AMAZING. ♥

I-I'M FINE.

HE LOOKED AWESOME IN HIS BLACK SUIT. ♥ I LOVED IT. ♥ ALL GUYS SHOULD WEAR BLACK SUITS!

SORRY, I FORGOT WHAT HE WAS WEARING. I THINK IT WAS SOMETHING LIKE THIS. PLEASE CHECK THE MAGAZINE.

HE WAS NOTHING LIKE HIS STAGE PERSONA, BUT HE WAS COOL ANYWAY. ♥

AND HE'S SO *DOWN-TO-EARTH!* HE'S NOT *STUCK UP* AT ALL! (I WAS SO SURPRISED!)

HE LOOKS SO *COOL* NO MATTER WHAT *CLOTHES* OR *MAKEUP* HE'S WEARING.

HE LISTENED TO EVERYTHING I SAID. ♥

SIGH... I WAS SO MOVED. ♥

LOTS OF MY FRIENDS ARE HUGE FANS.

I LOVED YOUR "SHONEN" CONCERT AT THE ZEPP TOKYO.

I FIGURED I'D NEVER GET A CHANCE LIKE THIS AGAIN, SO I SAT DOWN BY HIS FEET AND JUST KEPT TALKING TO HIM!

KYAA! ANOTHER DREAM COME TRUE. ♥

HE AUTO-GRAPHED ♥♥♥ MY DVD DURING HIS BREAK.

SOME OF MY READERS SENT ME RARE PHOTOS OF YOU FROM BACK WHEN YOU WERE JUST START-ING OUT.

THEY SEND ME CLIPPINGS TOO.

HE GAVE ME A DVD.

SORRY ABOUT ALL THAT BABBLING, KIYOHARU.

I BOUGHT TWO COPIES OF HIS PINUP PHOTO BOOK, JUST IN CASE I EVER GOT A CHANCE TO MEET HIM, BUT I FORGOT THEM BOTH...I'M SUCH AN IDIOT.

I TALKED ABOUT YOU GUYS TOO!

HE EVEN GAVE ME *SPECIAL TREATMENT.* ♥♥♥

IT WAS SO NICE OF HIM TO LET ME DO THAT. ♥

WHEN KIYOHARU-SAMA CAME OUT OF HIS DRESSING ROOM AFTER THE SHOOT, I ASKED HIM FOR A FAVOR...

SURE.

I'D LIKE TO THANK THE STAFF FROM FULL-FACE.

M-MAY I TAKE A PICTURE WITH YOU?

涙目。TEAR'S

AT THAT MOMENT, I DECIDED IT'S TIME FOR PLASTIC SURGERY.

HE WAS AT LEAST 20 CENTIMETERS TALLER THAN ME.

THANK YOU ZY-SAMA.

NOW I CAN LIVE HAPPILY EVER AFTER.

I'LL BE YOUR FAN FOREVER!

HE WAS SUCH A *SWEET, COOL SUPER HOTTIE!* ♥♥♥

LIFE IS FULL OF SURPRISES!

I WAS TRYING REALLY HARD NOT TO CRY. (I BROKE DOWN IN TEARS RIGHT AFTER-WARDS.)

HE SHOOK MY HAND BEFORE HE LEFT. ♥

《THE END》

THE OFFICIAL KIYOHARU WEBSITE
http://www.kiyoharu.jp

...SOME OF THE READERS MIGHT THINK THAT I DIDN'T SOUND NERVOUS AT ALL...

BUT THAT'S ONLY BECAUSE I DIDN'T REVEAL EVERYTHING SINCE I KNEW THIS MANGA WAS GONNA BE PUBLISHED IN *BESSATSU FRIEND*. IT WAS ACTUALLY MUCH, MUCH WORSE THAN I DESCRIBED. I WAS GOING CRAZY. I MEAN, WHAT COULD I DO? HE WAS SO GORGEOUS. ♥♥♥ I COULDN'T FIT EVERYTHING INTO FOUR PAGES. I COULDN'T REALLY PORTRAY HIS SEXINESS OR HIS VIBE IN THE DRAWINGS. ESPECIALLY HIS HUSKY, DEEP *VOICE*...EVERY SINGLE MOVEMENT HE MADE WAS COOL, AND IT'S NOT LIKE HE WAS TRYING OR ANYTHING...THAT MADE HIM EVEN COOLER. ♥

TO THIS DAY, IT STILL FEELS LIKE IT WAS ALL A DREAM.

I WAS ON THE VERGE OF BURSTING INTO TEARS ALL DAY, AND I WAS SAYING TO HAMANO-SAN (H-SAMA) THAT I MIGHT SOB IN THE TAXI ON THE WAY HOME. AND, AS SOON AS I LEFT THE STUDIO, I COULDN'T HOLD IT IN ANYMORE. I DIDN'T STOP CRYING UNTIL I GOT HOME. (THE TAXI DRIVER OFFERED ME A BOX OF TISSUES.) WHEN I GOT OUT OF THE TAXI, APPARENTLY I STARTED CROSSING THE STREET RIGHT THROUGH A RED LIGHT (ACCORDING TO HAMANO-SAMA).

IT MAKES ME CRY JUST THINKING ABOUT IT. I WAS REALLY, REALLY HAPPY. ♥♥♥

I READ THE INTERVIEW IN "ZY" WHEN IT CAME OUT. I WAS SURPRISED, BECAUSE IT TOTALLY LOOKED LIKE A REAL INTERVIEW. IT'S AMAZING WHAT WRITERS CAN DO. I SOUNDED COMPLETELY NORMAL.

IN THE MAGAZINE, I WAS LIKE...

YEAH, TOTALLY.

...THIS.

BUT IN REALITY, I WAS LIKE...

カチンコチン FROZEN

UH... UM...

...THIS.

I HAD A CHANCE TO TALK TO THE WRITER A LITTLE BIT, AND I THOUGHT, "THIS JOB WOULD BE A DREAM COME TRUE FOR FANS," BUT THEN I REALIZED THAT NO FAN COULD EVER HANDLE A JOB LIKE THIS. SHE WAS SUCH A COOL LADY. ♥

MY DREAM REALLY DID COME TRUE.

IT MADE ME REALIZE THAT DREAMS CAN ACTUALLY COME TRUE.

...NOW I DON'T HAVE ANY MORE GOALS IN LIFE...WHAT AM I GONNA DO? I'M CURRENTLY IN SEARCH OF A NEW DREAM.

I'M SERIOUS. MY DREAM REALLY WAS TO MEET KIYOHARU-SAMA IN PERSON...

IN SEPTEMBER, ♥ THE SAME MONTH I GOT TO INTERVIEW KIYOHARU-SAMA, ♥ I EXPERIENCED ANOTHER LIFE-CHANGING EVENT.

 I GOT A KITTY. ♥♥♥

I KEPT TRYING TO TALK MYSELF OUT OF GETTING A PET, BUT... IT WASN'T QUITE WORKING.

I MEAN, GIVE ME A BREAK. I TOTALLY WANTED A SCOTTISH CAT (OR A POMERANIAN), AND THEN A GOOD FRIEND OF MINE GOES AND GETS ONE AND STARTS TALKING ABOUT IT NONSTOP. (SHE HAD NO IDEA I WANTED A SCOTTISH SO BAD.) I ENVIED HER SO MUCH...(HER CAT IS REALLY SWEET.)

SO I WENT TO SEE SOME CATS, AND I PICKED THE CUTEST ONE OUT (I'M SO PICKY) AND TOOK HIM HOME. HE'S MUCH MORE AGGRESSIVE AND ACTIVE THAN MY FRIEND'S CAT, BUT HE'S JUST ADORABLE. I'M SO IN LOVE WITH HIM. HE BRINGS ME JOY EVERY DAY. ♥

I JUST WISH HE'D LET ME PICK HIM UP.

...HE HATES BEING PICKED UP, BUT HE LOVES TO BE OUT IN THE COLD... HE'S A LITTLE STRANGE.

I'VE GOT PLENTY OF "TEN" STORIES I'D LOVE TO SHARE. ♥ ...SORRY, I JUST LOVE MY KITTY SO MUCH...

*SORRY, I SUCK AT DRAWING CATS. I HOPE YOU CAN TELL HOW MUCH I LOVE HIM THOUGH....

THANK YOU FOR BUYING KODANSHA COMICS. ♥

EVER SINCE I WROTE ABOUT THE MISTAKE IN BOOK 8,
I'VE BEEN GETTING LETTERS FROM PEOPLE SAYING,
"I BOUGHT THE NEW VERSION." I FEEL BAD. I'M SORRY.
I HAD NO CONTROL OVER IT.
THANK YOU SO MUCH FOR HELPING TO CHEER ME UP.
YOU GUYS ARE GREAT.

"DAMN IT, I WANNA QUIT!" "AAHH, THIS IS TOO HARD!"
WHENEVER I FEEL THIS WAY (THAT'S PRETTY OFTEN THESE DAYS),
I READ YOUR LETTERS, AND THEY ALWAYS HELP MOTIVATE ME.
THEY MAKE ME FEEL 100 TIMES MORE POWERFUL.
I'M REALLY THANKFUL FOR THAT.

I HAVE NO PLANS TO START A WEBSITE, AND I HARDLY EVER
GO ONLINE (SORRY, I CAN'T KEEP UP WITH THE TECHNOLOGY),
SO THE ONLY WAY I CAN HEAR FROM YOU GUYS IS VIA OLD-
FASHIONED LETTERS.

LIKE I'VE SAID MANY TIMES BEFORE, THANK YOU SO MUCH
FOR YOUR SUPPORT. I PROMISE I WON'T LET YOU DOWN.

SPECIAL THANKS

HANA-CHAN

YOSHII

ARAKI-KUN

IYU KOZAKURA

MIZUHO AIMOTO-SENSEI

MACHIKO SAKURAI

MINE-SAMA

SHIOZAWA-SAMA

INO-SAMA

HAMANO-SAMA

EVERYBODY IN THE EDITING
DEPARTMENT

I JUST FOUND OUT THAT
YOU'RE GONNA BE WRITING
COMMENTS ON THE COVER
SLIP FOR THIS VOLUME ...

KIYOHARU-
SAMA.

THANK YOU VERY,
VERY MUCH.

About the Creator

Tomoko Hayakawa was born on March 4.

Since her debut as a manga creator, Tomoko Hayakawa has worked on many shojo titles with the theme of romantic love—only to realize that she could write about other subjects as well. She decided to pack her newest story with the things she likes most, which led to her current, enormously popular series, *The Wallflower*.

Her favorite things are: Tim Burton's *The Nightmare Before Christmas*, Jean-Paul Gaultier, and samurai dramas on TV. Her hobbies are collecting items with skull designs and watching *bishonen* (beautiful boys). Her dream is to build a mansion like the one the Addams family lives in. Her favorite pastime is to lie around at home with her cat, Ten (whose full name is Tennosuke).

Her zodiac sign is Pisces, and her blood group is AB.

Translation Notes

Japanese is a tricky language for most Westerners, and translation is often more art than science. For your edification and reading pleasure, here are notes on some of the places where we could have gone in a different direction in our translation of the work, or where a Japanese cultural reference is used.

Stomach warmer, page 15
What Yuki gives Kyohei is a *haramaki*, a kind of stomach warmer. It's a band of cloth worn around the stomach to help keep it warm.

Doraemon, page 22
Doraemon is one of Japan's most popular manga/anime characters. He's a magical, catlike creature.

Okonomiyaki, page 44
Okonomiyaki is a Japanese-style pancake filled with various kinds of meat and veggies.

Summers, page 65

Summers is a Japanese comedy group. The guys are also watching them on TV on page 4. The Summers comedians are famous for their ridiculous puns.

SMAP, page 82

SMAP is a very popular boy band.

Takoyaki, page 88

Takoyaki are octopus fritters. They taste much like *okonomiyaki*.

Bishonen, page 126
Bishonen is a term used to describe a cute young guy.

Takuya Kimura, page 126
Takuya Kimura, called "Kimitaku" for short, is a member of SMAP and one of Japan's most popular young male celebrities.

Preview of Volume 10

We're pleased to present you with a preview from volume 10. This volume will be available in English on November 28, 2006, but for now you'll have to make do with Japanese!

倒れたって？

大丈夫？

ぽと‥‥‥

あっ
スナコちゃーん

仮装リレーに
出場の方

登場ゲートに
集まってください

まずい……
まぶしいものに
あたりすぎた……

最後までもつかしら……

あの2人(ふたり)
なんで
あんなに
燃えてんの?

ねぇ

ね

そして
2人(ふたり)は
着々(ちゃくちゃく)と
1位(い)をとり

1

昼食(ちゅうしょく)もおわり
みなさんの
おなかも
こなれてきたころ

障害物競走

ヒュウウウウウ!

GENSHIKEN

The Society for the Study of Modern Visual Culture

BY KIO SHIMOKU

ARE YOU OTAKU?

It's the spring of freshman year, and Kanji Sasahara is in a quandary. Should he fulfill his long-cherished dream of joining an otaku club? Saki Kasukabe also faces a dilemma. Can she ever turn her boyfriend, anime fanboy Kousaka, into a normal guy? Kanji triumphs where Saki fails, when both Kanji and Kousaka sign up for Genshiken: The Society for the Study of Modern Visual Culture.

Undeterred, Saki chases Kousaka through various activities of the club, from cosplay and comic conventions to video gaming and collecting anime figures—all the while discovering more than she ever wanted to know about the humorous world of the Japanese otaku!

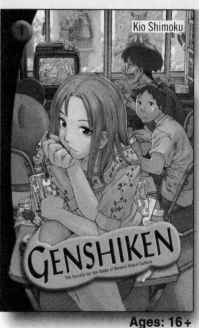

Ages: 16+

Special extras in each volume! Read them all!

Guru Guru Pon-Chan

BY SATOMI IKEZAWA

Ponta is a normal Labrador Retriever puppy, the Koizumi family's pet. Full of energy, she is always up to some kind of trouble. However, when Grandpa Koizumi, a passionate amateur inventor, creates the "Guru Guru Bone," which empowers animals with human speech, Ponta turns into a human girl!

Ponta dashes out into the street and is saved by Mirai Iwaki, the most popular boy at school! Her heart pounds and her face flushes. Why does she feel this way? Can there be love between a human and a dog?

The effects of the "Guru Guru Bone" are not permanent, and Ponta turns back and forth between dog and girl.

Ages: 13 +

Special extras in each volume! Read them all!

TOMARE!

止まれ
[STOP!]

You're going the wrong way!

Manga is a completely different type of reading experience.

To start at the *beginning*, go to the *end*!

That's right! Authentic manga is read the traditional Japanese way—from right to left. Exactly the *opposite* of how American books are read. It's easy to follow: Just go to the other end of the book, and read each page—and each panel—from right side to left side, starting at the top right. Now you're experiencing manga as it was meant to be!